C000291886

Francis Frith's
Around Leicester

PHOTOGRAPHIC MEMORIES

Francis Frith's
AROUND LEICESTER

Michael Kilburn
Inspector of Historic Buildings
English Heritage

First published in the United Kingdom in 2000 by
Frith Book Company Ltd

Hardback Edition
ISBN 1-85937-073-x

Paperback Edition 2001
ISBN 1-85937-381-x

British Library Cataloguing in Publication Data

Francis Frith's Around Leicester
Michael Kilburn

Frith Book Company Ltd
Frith's Barn, Teffont,
Salisbury, Wiltshire SP3 5QP
Tel: +44 (0) 1722 716 376
Email: info@francisfrith.co.uk
www.francisfrith.co.uk

Printed and bound in Great Britain

As with any historical database the Frith archive is constantly being corrected and improved
and the publishers would welcome information on omissions or inaccuracies

Contents

FRANCIS FRITH: *Victorian Pioneer*

FRANCIS FRITH, Victorian founder of the world-famous photographic archive, was a complex and multitudinous man. A devout Quaker and a highly successful Victorian businessman, he was both philosophic by nature and pioneering in outlook.

By 1855 Francis Frith had already established a wholesale grocery business in Liverpool, and sold it for the astonishing sum of £200,000, which is the equivalent today of over £15,000,000. Now a multi-millionaire, he was able to indulge his passion for travel. As a child he had pored over travel books written by early explorers, and his fancy and imagination had been stirred by family holidays to the sublime mountain regions of Wales and Scotland. 'What a land of spirit-stirring and enriching scenes and places!' he had written. He was to return to these scenes of grandeur in later years to 'recapture the thousands of vivid and tender memories', but with a different purpose. Now in his thirties, and captivated by the new science of photography, Frith set out on a series of pioneering journeys to the Nile regions that occupied him from 1856 until 1860.

INTRIGUE AND ADVENTURE

He took with him on his travels a specially-designed wicker carriage that acted as both dark-room and sleeping chamber. These far-flung journeys were packed with intrigue and adventure. In his life story, written when he was sixty-three, Frith tells of being held captive by bandits, and of fighting 'an awful midnight battle to the very point of surrender with a deadly pack of hungry, wild dogs'. Sporting flowing Arab costume, Frith arrived at Akaba by camel seventy years before Lawrence, where he encountered 'desert princes and rival sheikhs, blazing with jewel-hilted swords'.

During these extraordinary adventures he was assiduously exploring the desert regions bordering the Nile and patiently recording the antiquities and peoples with his camera. He was the first photographer to venture beyond the sixth cataract. Africa was still the mysterious 'Dark Continent', and Stanley and Livingstone's historic meeting was a decade into the future. The conditions for picture taking confound belief. He laboured for hours in his wicker dark-room in the sweltering heat of the desert, while the volatile chemicals fizzed dangerously in their trays. Often he was forced to work in remote tombs and caves where conditions were cooler. Back in London he exhibited his photographs and was 'rapturously cheered' by members of the Royal Society. His reputation as a photographer was made overnight. An eminent modern historian has likened their impact on the population of the time to that on our own generation of the first photographs taken on the surface of the moon.

Venture of a Life-Time

Characteristically, Frith quickly spotted the opportunity to create a new business as a specialist publisher of photographs. He lived in an era of immense and sometimes violent change. For the poor in the early part of Victoria's reign work was a drudge and the hours long, and people had precious little free time to enjoy themselves.

Most had no transport other than a cart or gig at their disposal, and had not travelled far beyond the boundaries of their own town or village. However, by the 1870s, the railways had threaded their way across the country, and Bank Holidays and half-day Saturdays had been made obligatory by Act of Parliament. All of a sudden the ordinary working man and his family were able to enjoy days out and see a little more of the world.

With characteristic business acumen, Francis Frith foresaw that these new tourists would enjoy having souvenirs to commemorate their days out. In 1860 he married Mary Ann Rosling and set out with the intention of photographing every city, town and village in Britain. For the next thirty years he travelled the country by train and by pony and trap, producing fine photographs of seaside resorts and beauty spots that were keenly bought by millions of Victorians. These prints were painstakingly pasted into family albums and pored over during the dark nights of winter, rekindling precious memories of summer excursions.

The Rise of Frith & Co

Frith's studio was soon supplying retail shops all over the country. To meet the demand he gathered about him a small team of photographers, and published the work of independent artist-photographers of the calibre of Roger Fenton and Francis Bedford. In order to gain some understanding of the scale of Frith's business one only has to look at the catalogue issued by Frith & Co in 1886: it runs to some 670

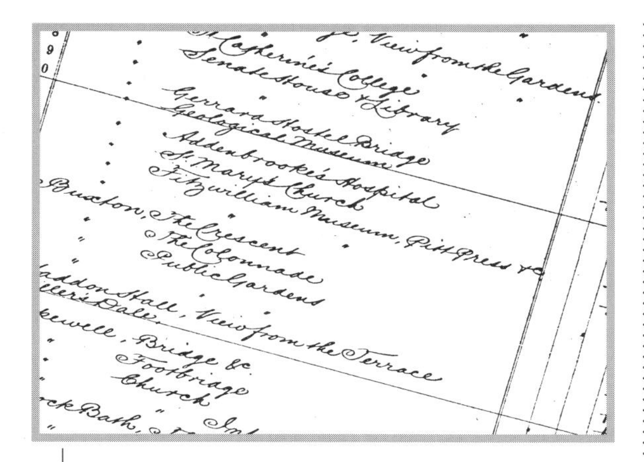
St Catherine's College, View from the Gardens
Senate House & Library
Gerrard Hostel Bridge
Geological Museum
Addenbrooke's Hospital
St Mary's Church
Fitzwilliam Museum, Pitt Press &c
Buxton, The Crescent
The Colonnade
Public Gardens
addon Hall, View from the Terrace
ller's Dale
kewell, Bridge &c.
Footbridge
Church

pages, listing not only many thousands of views of the British Isles but also many photographs of most European countries, and China, Japan, the USA and Canada – note the sample page shown above from the hand-written *Frith & Co* ledgers detailing pictures taken. By 1890 Frith had created the greatest specialist photographic publishing company in the world, with over 2,000 outlets – more than the combined number that Boots and WH Smith have today! The picture on the right shows the *Frith & Co* display board at Ingleton in the Yorkshire Dales. Beautifully constructed with mahogany frame and gilt inserts, it could display up to a dozen local scenes.

Postcard Bonanza

The ever-popular holiday postcard we know today took many years to develop. In 1870 the Post Office issued the first plain cards, with a pre-printed stamp on one face. In 1894 they allowed other publishers' cards to be sent through the mail with an attached adhesive halfpenny stamp. Demand grew rapidly, and in 1895 a new size of postcard was permitted called the court card, but there was little room for illustration. In 1899, a year after Frith's death, a new card measuring 5.5 x 3.5 inches became the standard format, but it was not until 1902 that the divided back came into being, with address and message on one face and a full-size illustration on the other. *Frith & Co* were in the vanguard of postcard development, and Frith's sons Eustace and Cyril continued their father's monumental task, expanding the number of views offered to the public and recording more and more places in Britain, as the coasts and countryside were opened up to mass travel.

Francis Frith died in 1898 at his villa in Cannes, his great project still growing. The archive he created continued in business for another seventy years. By 1970 it contained over a third of a million pictures of 7,000 cities, towns and villages. The massive photographic record Frith has left to us stands as a living monument to a special and very remarkable man.

Frith's Archive: *A Unique Legacy*

Francis Frith's legacy to us today is of immense significance and value, for the magnificent archive of evocative photographs he created provides a unique record of change in 7,000 cities, towns and villages throughout Britain over a century and more. Frith and his fellow studio photographers revisited locations many times down the years to update their views, compiling for us an enthralling and colourful pageant of British life and character.

We tend to think of Frith's sepia views of Britain as nostalgic, for most of us use them to conjure up memories of places in our own lives with which we have family associations. It often makes us forget that to Francis Frith they were records of daily life as it was actually being lived in the cities, towns and villages of his day. The Victorian age was one of great and often bewildering change for ordinary people, and though the pictures evoke an impression of slower times, life was as busy and hectic as it is today.

We are fortunate that Frith was a photographer of the people, dedicated to recording the minutiae of everyday life. For it is this sheer wealth of visual data, the painstaking chronicle of changes in dress, transport, street layouts, buildings, housing, engineering and landscape that captivates us so much today. His remarkable images offer us a powerful link with the past and with the lives of our ancestors.

See Frith at www. francisfrith.co.uk

Today's Technology

Computers have now made it possible for Frith's many thousands of images to be accessed almost instantly. In the Frith archive today, each photograph is carefully 'digitised' then stored on a CD Rom. Frith archivists can locate a single photograph amongst thousands within seconds. Views can be catalogued and sorted under a variety of categories of place and content to the immediate benefit of researchers. Inexpensive reference prints can be created for them at the touch of a mouse button, and a wide range of books and other printed materials assembled and published for a wider, more general readership - in the next twelve months over a hundred Frith local history titles will be published! The day-to-day workings of the archive are very different from how they were in Francis Frith's time: imagine the herculean task of sorting through eleven tons of glass negatives as Frith had to do to locate a particular sequence of pictures! Yet the archive still prides itself on maintaining the same high standards of excellence laid down by Francis Frith, including the painstaking cataloguing and indexing of every view.

It is curious to reflect on how the internet now allows researchers in America and elsewhere greater instant access to the archive than Frith himself ever enjoyed. Many thousands of individual views can be called up on screen within seconds on one of the Frith internet sites, enabling people living continents away to revisit the streets of their ancestral home town, or view places in Britain where they have enjoyed holidays. Many overseas researchers welcome the chance to view special theme selections, such as transport, sports, costume and ancient monuments.

We are certain that Francis Frith would have heartily approved of these modern developments, for he himself was always working at the very limits of Victorian photographic technology.

The Value of the Archive Today

Because of the benefits brought by the computer, Frith's images are increasingly studied by social historians, by researchers into genealogy and ancestory, by architects, town planners, and by teachers and schoolchildren involved in local history projects. In addition, the archive offers every one of us a unique opportunity to examine the places where we and our families have lived and worked down the years. Immensely successful in Frith's own era, the archive is now, a century and more on, entering a new phase of popularity.

The Past in Tune with the Future

Historians consider the Francis Frith Collection to be of prime national importance. It is the only archive of its kind remaining in private ownership and has been valued at a million pounds. However, this figure is now rapidly increasing as digital technology enables more and more people around the world to enjoy its benefits.

Francis Frith's archive is now housed in an historic timber barn in the beautiful village of Teffont in Wiltshire. Its founder would not recognize the archive office as it is today. In place of the many thousands of dusty boxes containing glass plate negatives and an all-pervading odour of photographic chemicals, there are now ranks of computer screens. He would be amazed to watch his images travelling round the world at unimaginable speeds through network and internet lines.

The archive's future is both bright and exciting. Francis Frith, with his unshakeable belief in making photographs available to the greatest number of people, would undoubtedly approve of what is being done today with his lifetime's work. His photographs, depicting our shared past, are now bringing pleasure and enlightenment to millions around the world a century and more after his death.

AROUND LEICESTER – *An Introduction*

THE PHOTOGRAPHS IN this volume do not embrace a wide spectrum of dates, being for the most part taken in 1955, when Sir Anthony Eden became Conservative Prime Minister and Manchester United won the Football League Championship, and 1965, highlighted by those early halcyon days of Harold Wilson's Labour Government and Manchester United, who again became League Champions.

In 1939, the author L T C Rolt, whose outstanding works include biographies of the great engineers Thomas Telford and Isambard Kingdom Brunel, bought 'Cressy', a converted narrow boat, and with his first wife set off to explore the intricate network of surviving canals, particularly around the Midlands. Setting out from Banbury on an exploration which was to last a year, 'Cressy' was pushed up the Grand Union Canal via Market Harborough and Foxton to enter Leicester through South Wigston, which Rolt referred to as ' a fragment of a city slum dropped in green fields', an acerbic comment which W G Hoskins was to echo some fifteen years later.

To Rolt, Leicester possessed only two memorable locations: firstly the open market, which appears to have been considerably more lively and colourful than he had ever anticipated, and secondly the church of St Mary de Castro, which to him serves as a memorial to the House of Lancaster, and is at the same time a treasure in building archaeological terms. It is only after these visits that Rolt wrongly comes to the conclusion that, along with other cities, ugliness and squalor underlie Leicester's superficial pomp and circumstance. As if as a final shot, he meets up with fishermen at Belgrave Lock on his way out of the city to find it full of dead rats, and draws the analogy between these 'malodorous corpses' and the city itself, an unforgivable slight.

Such generalisations based upon a superficial inspection are extremely difficult to support, but again Rolt refers, as a matter of course, to 'soot-blackened and pretentious public buildings', as well as 'mean streets where dwell the servants of the gas-works, mountainous refuse dumps, the power station and great mills'. He did not, at this date, recognise the quality of the city as an entity. His sensitivities are automatically geared towards buildings of the medieval period or perhaps a little later, even drifting to 1840, rather than the so-called Victorian buildings which compromise the greater part of the city. He, along with the vast majority of his contemporaries, appears to be only able to identify with recognisably ancient cities such as York or Canterbury and historic towns such as Warwick or Ludlow. In fact, it is only comparatively recently that Leicester has become recognised as one of the great 19th-century English cities, and its listing by the then Department of the Environment reflects this emphasis.

Between 1939 and 1955 the city changed remarkably little. Of course, Rolt probably arrived to see Charles Street being pushed through to ease the pressure of north/south traffic round the city centre. The shell of the rather forbidding Police Station at its southern end was probably in place, as was Lewis's store of 1936, and the Odeon cinema of 1938. The Second World War did not take such a tremendous toll on the city's buildings as it did in the cases of Coventry or Bristol; in fact Leicester lost no buildings of true architectural merit, so that in 1955, when this first series of photographs was taken, the pre-war city centre had changed little. But as the 1960s approached, the City Council, along with, it has to be said, most others, was overtaken by the irresistible urge to 'modernise'.

To exorcise itself of what the architectural world was telling it was ill-conceived Victorian rubbish, three very fine theatres were demolished, and streets of perfectly serviceable housing were lost; in their place came the faceless concrete or steel-framed buildings of the 1960s with which we are so familiar. I believe that had it not been for the government's introduction of the statutory listing process, Leicester's always less-than-sensitive

city council would happily have rid itself, along with its grammar schools, of the Grand Hotel, or Trubshaw's Midland Railway Station, or even the magnificent Town Hall, given only a breath of a chance. Evidence of the new architectural thinking is clearly recorded in two photographs of 1965: the rather dramatic but dated view of Lee Circle

car park, and the view looking at the northern end of Charles Street from Belgrave Gate approach.

It is no longer the omnipresent threat of demolition suspended over city centre buildings which gives most cause for concern in terms of preserving its character; it is, in my view, the forbidding task of regulating change in the sort of commercial world where for example, vast sheets of plate glass are considered preferable to the quality and design of traditional timber shop fronts. Almost every day good, if not 'old', shop fronts are wrenched out and abandoned to the skip, to make way for aluminium and plate glass awfulness. Sensitive signage is lost in a quest for bigger and bigger internally lit plastic fascias, and timber sliding sashed windows are abandoned to the smooth-talking pressure of the double-glazed plastic window salesmen. Perhaps the only blessing in all this is that stone cladding lost its appeal when house owners realised that it was more of an albatross than an asset.

We look at the photographs in this volume and we see, as we walk around the city, that the unified terraces and well-mannered buildings that existed in 1955 and 1965 have been turned into a peculiar mish-mash of plastic windows and doors, concrete interlocking tiles, painted brickwork, inappropriate brick pointing and, quite often, lost chimneystacks. The battle to regulate change is, to a great extent, being won where buildings are individually listed, but elsewhere, even in designated conservation areas, this is often not the case. Changes taking place are almost imperceptible, but where we are fortunate enough to be in possession of a dated series of photographs, we can monitor what usually amounts to an erosion of character, which is often exacerbated by the urge to 'neaten up' an area rather than allow it to evolve naturally. A particularly detrimental aspect of this 'neatening up' procedure is the removal of front boundary hedges and walls to make way for concreted or flagstoned hardstanding to accommodate at least one or maybe two cars. Strikingly missing from these photographs is the havoc wreaked on the townscape by the traffic engineer, whose obsession with signs and lines is bewildering in its intrusiveness.

Mid eighteenth-century Leicester remained a relatively small town, grouped within the line of the old town walls and retaining its basically mediaeval street pattern. Population was increasing from some six thousand at the beginning of the century to around ten thousand, and development was extending along North Gate, Humberstone Gate and South Gate, with the river demarcating the town's western boundary. All-in-all, it was a fairly normal town of the Georgian period. Sewage and water were always an ongoing problem until the mid 19th century, leaving us with the impression that the smell of the town would be lively and quite memorable. A self-employed scavenger could make a living on these 18th-century streets, and his direct descendant was vividly written of by Charles Dickens as the poor crossing sweeper in his novel 'Bleak House'.

During the 18th century turnpiking improved access by road, particularly to and from London, and in 1774 the town was opened up when its mediaeval gates were demolished. By the end of the century the canal had been extended to Leicester, which hastened the traffic of heavy goods. The end of the century also saw a phenomenon which was to have a devastating effect on the countryside: the enclosure of the open fields. A direct result of this was, in short, that many workers in agriculture were forced to seek alternative employment in towns.

The census of 1801 showed a town of some seventeen thousand people, a considerable increase on the 18th-century estimated figures. The hosiery industry flourished, and Leicester continued to expand, aided by the successful boot and shoe and engineering industries; the 1901 census put population figures at almost two hundred and twelve thousand people. The town expanded in a direct ratio to the numbers being absorbed; by the turn of the century, six Domesday villages within three miles of its centre had been engulfed - or, in the case of Humberstone, to the east of the town, were about to be engulfed in a second wave of expansion in the 1930s.

Humberstone is an excellent example of the erosion of character over an extended period. Just after the Second World War the village, which is basically aligned along a single street, possessed a Victorianised mediaeval church on its north side and a house which is known locally as the Manor House at its western end. Between them were two pubs, the plough, later the Humber Stone, a late 18th-century building, and The Windmill of about 1900, a post office, a small 19th-century village hall, and three general stores; perhaps more interestingly, at this date a blacksmith's shop survived, and local children could watch the grey smoke rise as horses were shod in the open yard. Also in the village, in a short three-storey row of red brick houses, was a shoe repairer, Mr Pick, who operated from a shop which could have dated from a hundred years earlier. Although relatively close to the city centre, the village retained a vague atmosphere of agriculture, particularly as the lands to the north and east were being farmed. Then the erosion began.

I have said previously that the city council, over the years, has shown little by way of architectural sensitivity or consideration beyond its need for money, and for better or worse it decided to build the large Netherhall Estate on the east side of the village, making encirclement complete. A not-unattractive row of 19th-century cottages was demolished to make way for up-to-the minute shops, the blacksmith disappeared and the shoe repairer, along with his wonderful shop, were both removed. The earlier pub was demolished and rebuilt in a bland style, and the Windmill pub has since been demolished to make way for housing. The village hall, small as it was, was deemed 'unsafe' and was demolished. This sad story of erosion is one that has been repeated round the city, and one which no doubt recurs throughout the country in the general and wider context. Although, with regret, we can print no comparative series of photographs which illustrates this slow downward transformation, I think the story of Humberstone is essential to any appreciation of the bigger picture of the expansion of the city at the cost of quality of life. As a postscript, it is worth recording the fate of a fine, small early 18th-century house to the east of the parish church, which was in use as a doctor's surgery until he moved on and the house became rundown rather than ruinous.

Instead of initiating a considered programme of rehabilitation and restoration, the council authorised its demolition and rebuilding. The rebuilding is worthy of attention in that it serves as a copybook example of how not to build in 'facsimile'. The new building is a naive pastiche of an original historic house that was once an asset to the village.

Since the visual disintegration of the village, a second huge bite has been taken out of the 'green belt' with the building of the so-called Hamilton Development. This is an unimaginative estate which has destroyed a swathe of the village's mediaeval pastures as it lurches on towards the particularly good deserted mediaeval village of Hamilton to its north. Humberstone is now connected to Thurmaston and on to Syston, and on again around the industrial estate-littered Ring Road.

The villages in this volume which lie outside the city's boundary are essentially confined to a group to its south and a second group to the north. A number have been, or continue to be, to a greater or lesser extent involved in the hosiery industry, or a direct offshoot of that industry, and that is reflected in the photographs, particularly those of Wigston and South Wigston, Syston, Countesthorpe and Fleckney. Others, such as Cossington, Newton Linford, Woodhouse Eaves and to an extent Kibworth Beauchamp, have retained an air of individuality divorced from the city, and just a breath of their agricultural past.

In one volume we have a snapshot of a Midland city at two important periods in its life. The first period was around 1955, when little had actually happened following the austerity of war; the second was around 1965, when development was well under way and a Brave New World could be seen quite clearly: a development often seen now, in retrospect, to have had regrettable and irreversible results.

In the face of councils who over the years have deprived the city of some of its finest buildings, abandoned schools of high education standing and will, without doubt, in due course abandon the county's centuries-old sporting traditions, God's own city and God's own county will survive - and long may they continue so to do.

CHAPTER ONE – *The City*

'God made the country and Man made the Town'

'The Task'. Book One. William Cowper (1731-1800)

THE FIRE STATION
Lancaster Road c1955 L144049
Along with the Ambulance Service, the Fire Brigade has earned and retained public respect. The City Headquarters building, designed in 1927 by A E and Trevor Sawday, encapsulates an air of civic authority whilst at the same time exhaling a breath of almost domestic-scale confidence in its brick and stone nine bay facade under a pitched pantile roof.

Wyggeston Girls' School c1950 L144030

The distinctive black and white uniforms of both the Wyggeston Boys' and Girls' Schools were in the 1950s and 1960s worn with a pride which said that along with Alderman Newton's School we are among the finest schools in the Midlands. The school building, designed by local architects Symington, Price and Pike in 1927 in a neo-Georgian manner, leans towards domesticity rather than scholarship.

The Memorial Gates, University Road c1965 L144115

Rising up Lancaster Road, away from the prison, the vista through to the City's War Memorial is broken by this magnificent set of wrought iron gates interspaced by stone piers crowned by vases. Dating from 1923, the gates and fixed railings comprise elaborate examples of the ironworkers' art in an 18th-century style. Beyond the gates and extending to the Memorial are formal flower gardens, shrubs and trees. On the London Road axis, gate lodges designed by Lutyens in the early 1930s mark the opening of a second vista to the memorial.

THE WAR MEMORIAL, VICTORIA PARK c1950 L144028
A drawing board, a tee-square, a blank sheet of cartridge paper and a commission to create a lasting memorial to the men of Leicester who gave their lives for freedom in the 1914-1918 war: an almost impossible task. It was the architectural genius Edwin Lutyens who faced that task and created a monument of great dignity and subtle beauty, whose presence ensures that neither the horrors nor the heroism of that conflict will be forgotten.

FIELDING JOHNSON BUILDING, UNIVERSITY OF LEICESTER c1965 L144112
Here we see a peaceful view of the campus at about the time of the completion of buildings of exceptional design quality, such as the Charles Wilson Building by Denys Lasdun and the Engineering Building by James Stirling and James Gowan; these helped to put Leicester into premier league contention. Wholly incongruous among these more modern structures, this brick-faced symmetrical building with its linked pavilions was in its former life the Leicestershire Lunatic Asylum of 1837, designed by a Mr Wallett and a Mr Parsons. This original use may be discernible in the closely-packed glazing bars to the ground storey windows of the pavilion.

De Montfort Hall, Regent Road c1955 L144118
As a spry 86-year-old, originally intended as a temporary structure, the De Montfort Hall shows little signs of ageing. Designed by Shirley Harrison in 1913 in a classical yet economical style, the rendered brick building sits well in its very formal garden, close to Victoria Park and to Lutyens' War Memorial. It is a tribute to that rare phenomenon, the architect who can produce an all round first-rate building on a limited budget.

De Montfort Hall, Regent Road c1955 L144125
A very loose use of classical elements has produced, under an impressive barrel vault, seemingly supported on outsize brackets, one of the Midlands' finest concert halls. Cantilevered balconies ensure clear visibility, while the acoustics are excellent. Over the years the Hall has heard and seen almost every kind of performance, ranging from Pavlova to Liberace and from Ted Heath to Rock and Roll. It has played host to many city school speech days.

THE PAVILION, VICTORIA PARK, LONDON ROAD c1965 L144109
In direct contrast to the Pavilion by James Tate in Abbey Park, here is a brick and render symmetrical watered-down vision of the future as seen through the eyes of the Council of the early 1960s in Victoria Park. It is regrettable that the Pavilion is clearly visible from London Road as one arrives from the south, and it may be that a tree screen could be considered helpful.

THE POLICE STATION, CHARLES STREET c1950 L144045
This is an austere, almost threatening building, in an English Palazzo style, hardly the imagined face of the friendly local 'Bobby'. With its rusticated ground storey and ashlar-faced upper storeys, designed by Noel Hill in 1933, it fails to match in design quality other police stations such as Hammersmith by Donald McMorran, 1938 or even Savile Row by Burnet, Tate and Lorne, 1939. Whether by design or accident, the building suggests that some difficulty could be encountered by anyone trying to leave.

Charles Street c1950 L144044
A swish, up-to-the-minute dual carriageway was created to relieve the pressure of excessive traffic in 1931 by widening and extending a street which, until that time, ran only between Humberstone Gate and Rutland Street. On the left of the photograph are survivors of the late 19th/ early 20th century looking across to poorly designed buildings of the 1930s. Charles Street has never developed as a shopping street, having always been a rather sad throughway.

Charles Street c1955 L144057
When Charles Street was widened and extended, a great opportunity was lost to introduce buildings and shopping of quality. Instead, as seen in this photograph, which records the new extension northwards from Humberstone Gate, the buildings are modest, almost retiring, while the Council's attention to streetscape amounts to a concrete flower trough. Lea's Clock was always a useful reference as a meeting place.

CHARLES STREET AND BELGRAVE GATE c1965 L144095
Here it is at the northern end of Charles Street, the architects' and planners' vision of utopia a la 1950s and 60s; dominating the photograph to the left, in a Midlands-Miesian style, is Epic House of 1963 by Andrews, Emmerson and Sherlock. It becomes difficult to imagine what was said at the council's Planning Committee Meeting when it granted consent to the three-storey eyesore in the centre of the shot, and even more so when it is remembered that the same committee was, at about that time, taking the monstrous decision to authorise the demolition of the 18th-century Theatre Royal, the Palace Theatre and the Opera House, three Leicester buildings of national importance.

HUMBERSTONE GATE C1949 L144007

How well-ordered the wide street scene appears as it curves away towards Uppingham, with virtually no cars, only rumbling trams and plenty of buses. Little survives of the original 18th-century development apart from the Bell Hotel in the middle distance. The small scale of the buildings on the left of the shot, the varying eaves height, and the mix of materials does, however, go some way to perpetuate an echo of those early days. The quirky Art Deco of Lewis's store on the right manages not to detract from the overall friendliness of the immediate area. It is regrettable that a high proportion of the buildings in this photograph have been demolished in recent years.

RAPID
SMITHS
TOBACCONIST

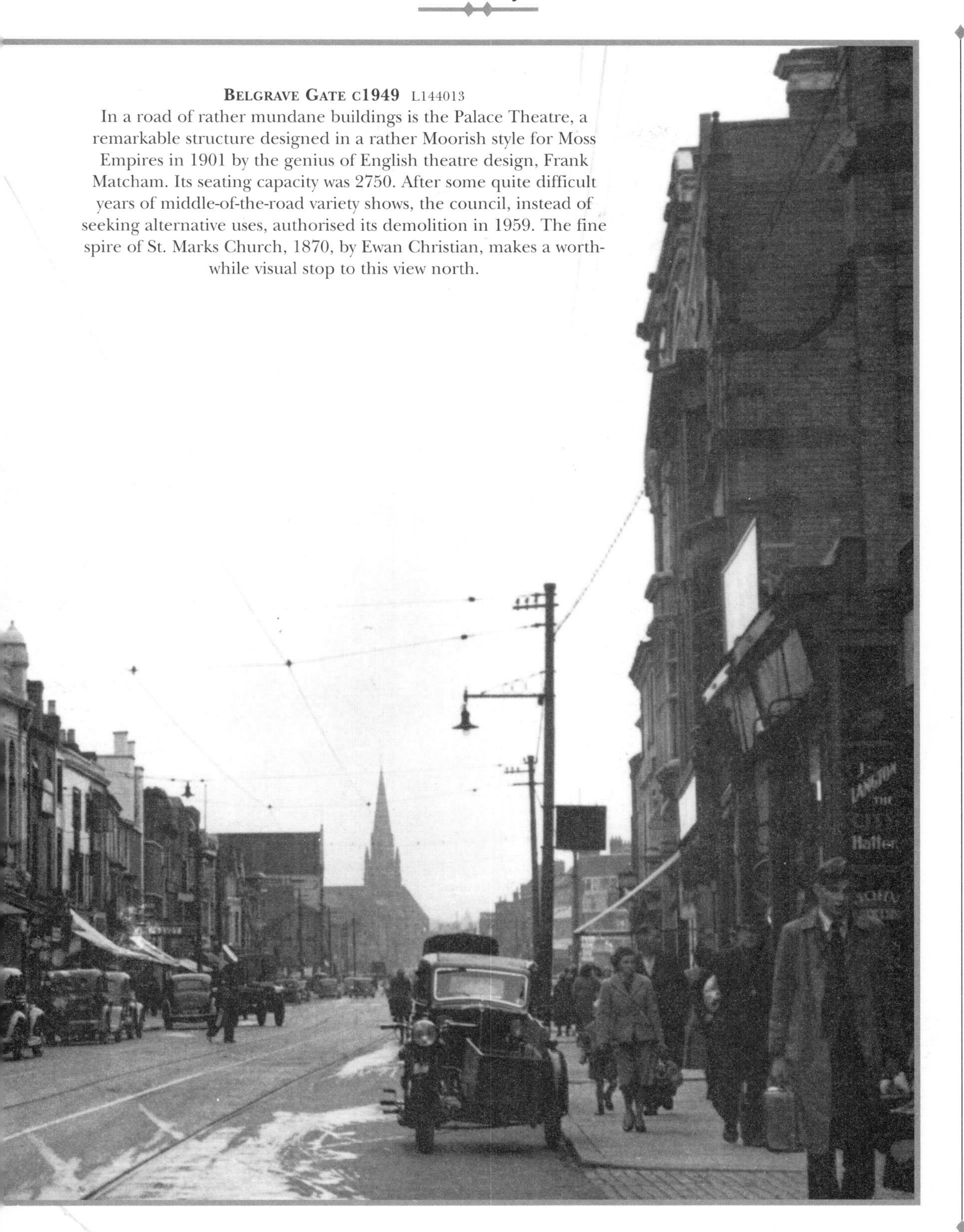

Belgrave Gate c1949 L144013

In a road of rather mundane buildings is the Palace Theatre, a remarkable structure designed in a rather Moorish style for Moss Empires in 1901 by the genius of English theatre design, Frank Matcham. Its seating capacity was 2750. After some quite difficult years of middle-of-the-road variety shows, the council, instead of seeking alternative uses, authorised its demolition in 1959. The fine spire of St. Marks Church, 1870, by Ewan Christian, makes a worthwhile visual stop to this view north.

EAST GATE AND THE CLOCK TOWER c1950 L144011
The pinnacled and canopied Clock Tower, designed by Joseph Goddard in 1868, dominates the forefront of the photograph, while its four stoney local worthies, Simon de Montfort, William Wyggeston, Alderman Gabriel Newton and Sir Thomas White, Mayor of Leicester and mine host at the nearby Horse and Trumpet, gaze down. Beyond Corts Limited can be seen the dominant dome of the Opera House, demolished in 1960, where each year the Christmas pantomime was staged and appreciated with thunderous applause by generations of children.

THE CLOCK TOWER AND GALLOWTREE GATE c1965 L144097
Looking southwards from the Haymarket into Gallowtree Gate: it is the building immediately to the left of the Clock Tower which is of interest. A quite spectacular new front of 1894 was added to an older building, recording that from these offices Mr Thomas Cook arranged the world's first cheap day rail excursion (to Loughborough) in 1841, and went on to provide affordable travel for ordinary people, both at home and on the continent. He died in 1892, a stalwart of the Temperance Movement, but at the same time a man who has given much pleasure to the world.

AUTO MAGIC CAR PARK, LEE CIRCLE c1965 L144087
Situated behind the Palais de Dance, off Humberstone Gate, and incorporating an early supermarket and ten pin bowling facility, the six levels of Lee Circle car park were intended to relieve the city of what even in the early 60s was becoming a problem: an excess of the motor car. Multi-storey car parks are, like bungalows, notoriously difficult to design, but the tremendous horizontality of the protective concrete walls produces a dramatic, almost nautical response to a difficult brief.

GALLOWTREE GATE c1950 L144009
Gallowtree Gate runs out of Granby Street and London Road as it drops down to the Clock Tower. Its derivation is probably literal, in that it may well refer to the gallows which were sited at the top of London Road hill, close to its junction with Evington Lane. Like much of Leicester, the photograph shows an intelligent use of the classical vocabulary without excitement or grandeur. In the 15th century, Gallowtree Gate and Church Gate ran parallel with the east wall of the town and the town ditch.

Granby Street 1949 L144031

The link between London Road and Gallowtree Gate, this short north-south road is visually of the later 19th century. The Grand Hotel of 1898 by Cecil Ogden (1858-1944) dominates its southern end, while the rather exuberant Turkey Cafe of 1901 by Arthur Wakerley and the Victoria Coffee House of 1888 by Edward Burgess (fl.1886-1915) add that longed-for touch of eccentricity and quality to an otherwise undistinguished townscape. The shops to the left of the photograph retain their excellent fronts with stall-boards and timber frames, a sight which has become a rarity in a plate-glass world.

THE TOWN HALL c1950 L144023
The early 19th century saw Leicester in an appalling sanitary condition, until piped water came to the town in the mid 1850s, along with its first sewers. After the piped water and the sewers came the benevolent face of bureaucracy in the new brick-faced Town Hall, designed by local architect F J Hames in 1876 in a friendly yet impressive Queen Anne style, on the western side of its open square.

THE TOWN HALL GARDENS c1965 L144099
In 1965 the birds still sang in the Town Hall gardens, and although relatively noisy, it was an extremely pleasant place to sit and mull over the fortunes of the day. Dominated by the Town Hall on its west side, and sheltered by trees and hedges, sandwiches could be consumed and pigeons fed on the crusty remnants. Hairgrip fencing, that universal symbol of municipal parks, adds a slightly discordant, keep-off-the-grass note to the scene.

The Town Hall Gardens c1965 L144100
Presented with a fine bronze circular fountain adorned with four winged lions and set centrally within the square, it is surprising that the garden's designer could resist the temptation to continue the circular theme. Seen here from the tower of the Town Hall, the rather bulbous layout (which, it has to be said, is less noticeable from eye level) could, with imagination, have been improved so as to relieve the 50-50 tarmac/grass solution.

Town Hall Square c1965 L144103
This photograph, taken from the tower of the Town Hall, looks down past the formal square to the buildings of Bishop Street, which include the reference library by Edward Burgess of 1904 and the former Liberal Club, also by Burgess, of 1888. In a street of attractive buildings the eyecatcher is prominent to the right of the photograph: the fine, classical brick-faced Methodist Church of 1815 by the Rev. William Jenkins (1763-1844). Having retired from the ministry in 1810, Jenkins practised as an architect in London, designing chapels with a touch of brilliance from Exeter to Darlington.

THE COLLEGE OF ART AND TECHNOLOGY
The Newarke c1965 L144090

In 1955 the College of Art and Technology was soon to be uplifted to the status of a Polytechnic. This main building, which stands close to the Castle site and the early 15th-century Magazine Gateway, was designed by local architects Everard and Pick (later Pick, Everard, Keay and Gimson) around 1896, with an economic lack of detail. Here a whole range of non-university subjects could be studied, ranging from architecture to sculpture, and from surveying to interior design. Under the building are fragments of the Hospital of the Annunciation of the Virgin Mary which was founded in 1330, but in 1355 Henry, Duke of Lancaster, refounded it as a secular college. Notwithstanding this change, it continued to care for fifty poor men, fifty poor women, and ten nursing sisters until it was dissolved in 1548.

PRINCE RUPERT'S GATEWAY AND ST MARY DE CASTRO CHURCH c1955 L144050
A prominent Norman castle mound, the remains of the town walls, including Prince Rupert's Gateway, the castle hall and St Mary de Castro church form the finest historic enclave in the city. The Gateway, seen here from the Newarkes, was ruined around 1832, having survived the siege of the town by Prince Rupert and King Charles I in 1645. The group is of considerable beauty, and no visitor should fail to perambulate and absorb the whole of this amazingly compact historic group of buildings and earthworks.

THE TUDOR GATEHOUSE, CASTLE STREET c1955 L144093

THE TUDOR GATEHOUSE
Castle Street c1955

This attractive close-studded timbered house of the mid 15th century provides a fine, almost secret entrance to Castle Yard. Sited on the north west angle of the Church of St Mary de Castro, and opposite the Norman Great Hall, the whole ambience stirs feelings of regret that just a little more of early Leicester could not survive.

THE GREAT HALL
Castle Yard c1965

The Great Hall, built by Robert, Earl of Leicester around 1150, cannot compare with that of Oakham Castle of c1180, some twenty miles east of the city, as an example of Norman architecture; but as part of the extensive remains of Leicester Castle and its town defences, it is quite remarkable. Although the building has been pared down from its original aisled form, and has been provided with what is basically a 17th-century range and brick front, enough original fabric remains to render the structure important in a European context. Since the turn of the 14th century and extending into the 20th century, the Hall has been in court use. The photograph shows a small group of policemen, probably waiting to give their evidence!

THE GREAT HALL, CASTLE YARD c1965 L144092

THE GUILDHALL

Guildhall Lane c1965 L144086

Leicester grew rapidly in the 18th and 19th centuries, but it continued to be governed from its small medieval Guildhall until 1876. Situated among the somewhat reduced remnants of Georgian Leicester, now tightly grouped in New Street, Peacock Lane and Friar Lane, the building is overshadowed by St Martin's Cathedral (upgraded in 1927 from parish church status). To the rear is the former Alderman Newton's Boys Grammar School, the resited 18th-century foundation of Alderman Gabriel Newton, who lies buried in the churchyard of All Saints, High Cross Street. With its amazing 14th-century timbered Great Hall of the Corpus Christi Guild, the building is open to the public, and will reward the short walk from the city centre.

THE JEWRY WALL c1955 L144069
The extensive remains of Ratae Coritanorum, the origins of the city, and a Roman regional capital, are not only to be seen exposed on the surface, but extend under surrounding buildings. The so-called Jewry Wall, which can be seen in front of the superb Saxon Church of St Nicholas, formed a part of the exercise hall to the public bath. The site was excavated in the 1930s by Dame Kathleen Kenyon, but it has managed to remain a comparatively unsung part of Roman history. The remains are situated at the top of High Street and are, in my view, a must for the first-time visitor to the city.

Cavendish House

Abbey Park c1955 L144088

This house of 1600 was built by Henry Hastings, Earl of Huntingdon, using stone robbed from the remains of Leicester Abbey; but it was to be reduced to a skeletal ruin by fire 45 years later. The main front seen in the photograph is virtually all that remains; the house to the right is 19th century. The Abbey of St Mary de Pratis, which is laid out in the north-west angle of the park, was one of the largest in England of the Augustinian Order. It was founded in 1143 by Robert le Bossu, and was dissolved in 1538 after an unsuccessful attempt by the last abbot to withstand the suppression. At the end, the Abbey had a very large annual income in excess of £950, and twenty monks were pensioned off. The Abbey ruins are presently (1999) included in English Heritage's Register of Buildings at Risk.

THE PAVILION, ABBEY PARK c1965 L144089
A Pavilion by James Tait (1834-1915), typical of the early 1880s, with its hints of Gothic merging into Tudor framing, making a valuable contribution to the ambience of the park, which was laid out in 1882. In this case, the formality of the rose garden enhances rather than detracts from the symmetry of the building.

ABBEY PARK c1950 L144039
Sham timbered lodges and a refreshment pavilion graced the newly-laid-out park, and mature trees retained from the Abbey Fields formed an essential part of the emparkment scheme. Into this somewhat irregular setting were inserted the drawing-board creations of formal, manicured rose gardens with their inevitable stone urns and steps leading down from a parterre.

The Band Stand, Abbey Park c1955 L144058

Bandstands are, by their very nature, fascinating pieces of municipal equipment. Very rarely are they to be found in use, but nevertheless they seem to generate vivid images of Victorian England at peace with itself, nannies with prams exercising in the park, and lovers sitting entranced by red-coated bandsmen. This rather weedy example has a touch of the orient built into its roof, but as usual it sits in silence.

The Lake, Abbey Park c1955 L144059

What is there more pleasurable than to take a rowing boat out onto a picturesque, well-treed lake, to escape for an afternoon of peace and relaxation away from Leicester's factories and mills? Although the park has been municipalised, it is an essential green lung which must never be forfeited to any so-called development pressures under any circumstances.

CHAPTER TWO – *The Churches*

What is a church? - Our honest sexton tells.
'Tis a tall building, with a tower and bells.

'The Borough'. Letter 11-The Church. George Crabbe (1754-1832)

ANSTEY

St Mary's Church c1965 A312016

Raised above the road, behind a rather forbidding local stone boundary wall, the rather stumpy three-stage crenellated west tower is all that remains of the medieval church. The remainder was rebuilt in 1846 to their own designs by a firm of local builders, Broadbent and Hawley, in an admirable and quite professional fashion. There is little of architectural interest to be found inside the building.

COSBY, ST MICHAELS CHURCH c1965 C433004

Situated at what is now the southern end of this expanded village, the church with its elegant recessed spire dates for the greater part from the earlier 15th century. An oddity is the large external projection which houses the rood loft staircase; evidence suggests that the fabric of the chancel may predate the body of the church. God's breath will not be allowed to ripple the grassy sepulchral mounds of generations of villagers in this chaste churchyard.

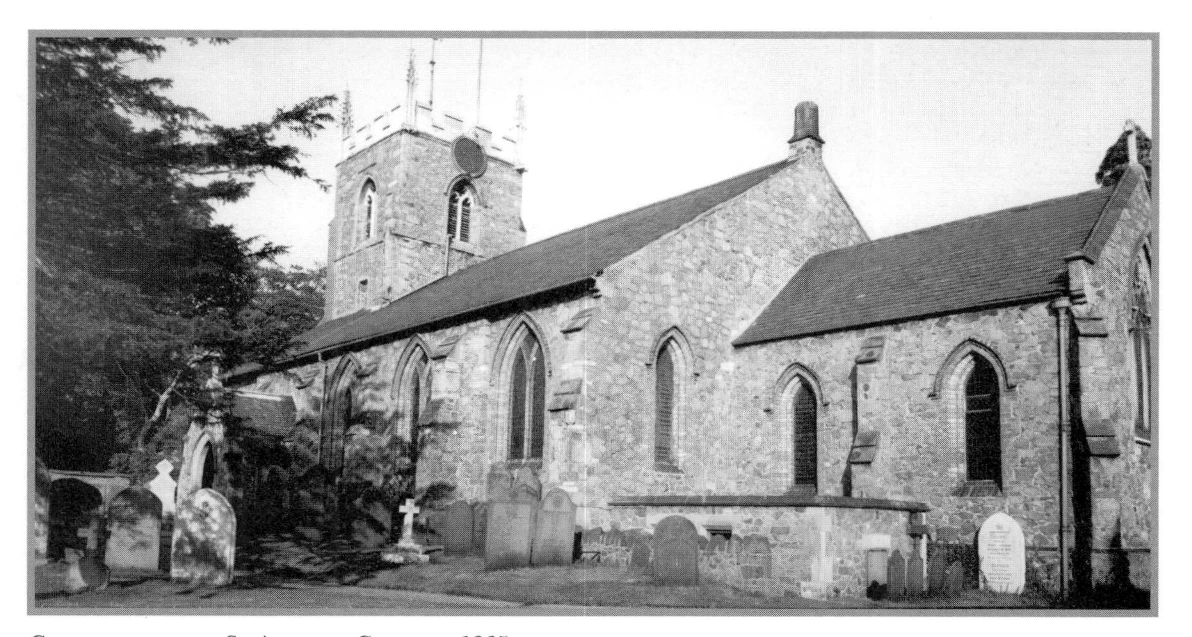

COUNTERSTHORPE, ST ANDREWS CHURCH c1965 C471012

The original heart of this sprawling village, the battlemented tower is the complete surviving remnant of the medieval church. The remainder of this oddly proportioned building was designed or altered by Henry Goddard, a prolific Leicester architect, in the early 1840s. His son Joseph, a rather more talented designer, was responsible for the city's Clock Tower in 1868.

EARL SHILTON, ST SIMON AND ST JUDE c1965 E161303
Visible evidence of medieval Sultan is sparse, but remnants of the castle motte survive to the west of the parish church. Once on the edge of Leicester Forest, this visually undistinguished town became in the 19th century a focal point of the framework knitting industry. The medieval four-stage tower of the church with its recessed crocketted spire dates from around 1400, but the remainder of the building is good High Victorian work, in the main by Richard Cromwell Carpenter (1812-1855), architect of Lancing College, Sussex (1854) and Inverness Cathedral (1855).

GROBY, CHURCH OF ST PHILIP AND ST JAMES, MARKFIELD ROAD c1960 G220001
The church, which dates from 1840, lies to the south of the castle motte, and close to the busy A50 bypass. Raised well above the road, with its emaciated battlemented tower and unimaginative body, it was designed by William Railton (c1801-1877), who was at the time Architect to the Ecclesiastical Commissioners and the designer of Nelson's Column in Trafalgar Square. The two-bay Chancel was added in 1912.

KIBWORTH BEAUCHAMP, CHURCH OF ST WILFRED c1955 K119011
Close to the road, the solid but impressive ashlar tower dominates the immediate street scene with its substantial angled buttresses and crocketted finials; these are not 15th-century, but were added in 1832, after the collapse of the original tower, by the local architect William Flint (1801-1862), whose specialism was Greek Revival. The body of the church is fairly run-of-the-mill with its four-bay nave arcade, but it does house some 19th-century stained glass of interest. The usual Victorian 'restoration' was carried out by William Slater (1819-1872) in 1860.

KIRBY MUXLOE, ST BARTHOLOMEW'S CHURCH c1965 K126002
A pleasant enough small church, set as a church should be in grassy, tombed surroundings, well populated by recumbent villagers. The body of the church is 14th century, but any patina of age was effectively neutralised by the over-restorations of 1849 and 1857. The added tower enhances the overall composition, but should the church be locked, an extended search for the key is not justified.

LEICESTER, ST MARGARET'S CHURCH, ST MARGARET'S WAY c1955 L144068
Situated just outside the Inner Ring Road on the north side of the city, St Margaret's, one of Leicestershire's finest mainly 15th-century churches, can hardly be said to be enhanced by its factory and bus station setting. It is externally impressive, and internally large and light, with perhaps the too-overwhelming feeling that the hand of the Victorian restorer has been somewhat heavy. There are some unattributed monuments, and modest glass, but all is just a fraction too bland. The other building, which occupies a high percentage of this shot, has the turn-of-the-century feel of E.S. Prior about it.

LEICESTER, ST MARTIN'S CATHEDRAL c1955 L144026
Sited away from the city centre in the last remaining enclave of 18th-century and earlier buildings, the Cathedral with its fine broach spire of 1862 would hardly wring an awed gasp from even the most god-fearing postulant. Raised to Cathedral status in 1927, the building, although exhibiting 13th-century fabric, exudes an air of Victorian England, for it was 'restored' and added to by such hallowed names as George Edmund Street and J L Pearson in the 1880s and 1890s. Its monuments, including one by Joshua Marshall to John Whatton (1656), are worthy of inspection.

LEICESTER, ST MARY DE CASTRO CHURCH c1955 L144070

LEICESTER
St Mary de Castro Church c1955

St.Mary de Castro, situated as its name implies within the medieval castle, was founded by Robert de Beaumont in 1107 as a secular college, but by c1143 it had been annexed to Leicester's large Augustinian abbey. Although much restored in the 19th century, and its spire rebuilt in 1785, it is pleasing if not quite spectacular. Internally the church is an exercise in building archaeology rather than a thing of great beauty. A visit to St Mary's is a must for anyone who has not already done so, accompanied by an up-to-date copy of Pevsner.

NEWTOWN LINFORD
All Saints Church c1965

Prominent on the north side of Bradgate Road as it rises away from the City towards Ulverscroft Priory, the church with its recessed spire is comparatively unadorned, apart from a large 15th-century traceried window on its south side. The north aisle and stubby chancel were added by local architects Harry Roberts and John Woodhouse Simpson in 1895. The interior is not without interest.

NEWTOWN LINFORD, ALL SAINTS CHURCH c1965 N96002

ROTHLEY, CHURCH OF ST MARY AND ST JOHN THE BAPTIST c1965 R259014
A tranquil setting for a fine pink granite church, mainly of the 15th century, with its solid buttressed and battlemented tower rising in four stages. The chancel was added by J Reynolds Rowe as part of an overall 'restoration' programme in 1877. There are a number of monuments, including one in memory of Anne Babinton of 1648, possibly by Edward Marshall, whose eldest son Joshua produced a very good signed monument which can be seen on the north side of the Cathedral.

SMEETON WESTERBY, CHRIST CHURCH, SADDINGTON ROAD c1955 S742007
The village, which in parochial terms was originally bracketed together with Kibworth Beauchamp and Kibworth Harcourt, which share the mother church of St Wilfred, lies some eight miles to the south of the city. Sited on the southern edge of the village, the small church of 1849 was designed by Henry Woodyer in a 14th-century manner; whilst quite pretty, it cannot be said to be of great architectural moment. In fact, its west end, seen in the photograph, gives the false impression that the grand nave arch has been blocked following the demolition of more elaborate fabric.

CHAPTER THREE – *The Villages*

O Charnwood, be thou called the choicest of thy kind,
The like in any place, what flood hath happed to find?
No tract in all this isle, the proudest let her be,
Can show a sylvan nymph for beauty like to thee.

'Charnwood Forest'
Michael Drayton. (1563-1631)

ANSTEY
Pack Horse Bridge c1965 A312002
The 16th-century stone bridge steps quietly by way of its five arches across the reedy Rothley Brook; the original roadway into the village is now reduced to a footpath. Isolated, as the road now crosses the water to its north, the bridge seems to take about itself an air of romance, probably associated with the image of luxury-laden animals in fact, their loads rarely amounted to anything more than day-to-day necessities.

Anstey, The Nook c1965 A312009

It is said that the first rumblings of the Luddite Movement were felt in Anstey with the breaking of the knitting frames; the village had expanded rapidly to accommodate an influx of workers. The picture clearly shows Anstey's 19th-century growth with a quite picturesque composition of tiled roofs and stacks. The National Provincial Bank, as banks do, took advantage of this 'additional wealth', followed later by Doug Taylor's garage and the inevitable council roundabout.

Anstey, The Nook c1965 A312008

Although the scene is basically little changed, apart from the loss of the National Provincial Bank on the right (it was replaced by an archetypal building of the 1960s or early 1970s, larger but of lesser merit), the Nook sparkles rather more 35 years later than it did when the photograph was taken.

ANSTEY, BRADGATE ROAD c1965 A312011
The view shows the centre of Domesday Anstige, as the road drops down from the heights of Bradgate Park. Much redbrick building of the 19th century has intruded into the village scene as industry spread from Leicester, including the impressive backdrop of the factory building against the more domestic shops. Along with its more recent arrivals, Anstey does retain some vestiges of its less recent past in a small collection of timber-framed buildings.

BILLESDON, THE MARKET PLACE c1955 B593002
An excellent small history of the village has recently been published by the Local History Group, which looks in the main at Billesdon's evolution since the 18th-century enclosures. Oblong in plan, with the church at its southern end and the A47 to the north, the village is entered by long-abandoned medieval roads from Cold Newton to the north, itself a shrunken village, and from Gaulby and Frisby to the south-west. Best seen on foot, the village is attractive without being pretty, offering a wide range of vernacular buildings and a topographical conundrum in sequencing its development. Allow time to absorb this multi-faceted village at leisure.

COSBY

Croft Road from The Nook c1965 C433009

Cosby presents a most unusual configuration for a Leicestershire village, which with care and attention over the years could have been described as picturesque. The openness of the village centre is striking, with some good later 18th/early 19th-century houses ranging either side of the grass-banked brook, with its modest urban district council railings and finger post. In the background is a substantial brick and timber framed barn dated 1766 - this is the date of the brickwork, the timbering being considerably older. As so often happens in the county, the quality of the village has gone unsung, with the brook, its major natural asset, now being forced between crazy-paved walls instead of gently enhanced - a pity. In Forryan Close a framework knitting shop survives.

COSBY

Main Street c1965 C433006

This photograph, looking towards The Nook, highlights the frustration of what could have been. The arid area of grass and the 1950s housing (both family and sheltered) could, with a lightness of touch, have provided a more special entrance to the village from the north, under the shadow of St Michael's Church. Instead, little has happened since 1965, except that the spindly trees on the right have matured and The Huntsman pub (previously The New Inn) has been rebuilt in a bland red brick. In 1615 the vicar complained bitterly that he could not support his family on a wage of under five pounds a year, and now, as a visitor, I felt that it is the very fabric of the village that seems to be echoing his sentiment.

COSSINGTON, THE VILLAGE c1965 C470002

An oasis between industrial Syston and unlovely Sileby, the scene has changed little over the years, apart from a stepping-up in volume of motorised traffic. In the village are a good variety of houses, including the early 16th-century rectory and Hallside Grove, a Gothicised house of quality set behind the low wall on the left of the photograph. Thank God that 19th- and 20th-century blight has somehow failed to desecrate Cossington.

COSSINGTON, THE VILLAGE c1965 C470001

Built about the time that Jane Austen was writing in Hampshire, the simple but attractive farm house on the left graces a peaceful well-treed rural villagescape. Immediately beyond, modern infill points the way towards the fully-developed commuter dormitory scenario soon to be fully exploited in a tightly-drawn belt around the city.

Countesthorpe, Main Street c1965 C471013
Few buildings remain which pre-date the Enclosure Acts, effectively extinguishing the ties within rural communities in much of Leicestershire, and indeed the Midland counties. At the head of the street, the white cottage of the later 16th century is one of few survivors, built prior to Enclosure in 1767. The remainder step down the street in chronological order: later 19th-century shops, and the Bull's Head Pub built around the turn of the century. Countesthorpe is an industrialised village of very mixed architectural fortunes.

Countesthorpe, Station Road c1965 C471024
The road extends to the now defunct railway line as 20th-century Countesthorpe balloons in an amoebic sprawl westwards towards Cosby and Whetstone. In the residual hedgerows and trees lie clues to an 18th-century rural landscape; the enclosures of the 1760s were hated by John Clare, the Northamptonshire poet, for its deleterious effect on the lives of ordinary village people, and for its destruction of the open fields.

Fleckney

High Street looking South-East c1960 F134013

In place before the Conquest, Fleckney continues to develop and extend with a population of 71 in 1381 increasing by 1950 to nearly 1500 - and the increase goes on. This photograph shows a village opening out onto the low hedges and standard trees of the 1769 enclosure fields, which in their turn overlie the prominent ridge and furrow of an earlier age. From the camera's viewpoint little has changed. The shop with its attractive front remains in post office use, and the other buildings have new plastic windows; but stopping the long view, without being intrusive, is a new estate of houses, slowly, slowly changing the character of Leicestershire's semi-rural scene.

FLECKNEY

High Street looking North-West c1960 F134018

The good, the bad and the ugly is a phrase which springs to mind as one looks up the High Street. W G Hoskins refers to Fleckney as 'a large and dreary industrial village', but I would hesitate to go totally down that road. A hosiery village it might have been, but the High Street retains much of the quiet charm shown in the photograph, apart from the demolition of key vista-stopping cottages. On the right is Brookside, abutted by a decent brick-fronted house with its later bungalow shop. It is here that the ugly appears, in the form of a hot red-brick building probably of the 1970s or 80s in use as a Baptist church, totally obliterating the lane. Were no voices raised in protest when this building was submitted to the local Planning Committee?

Fleckney, Kilby Road c1960 F134011
When factories arrived in the village in the 19th century, ribbon development along the Wistow, Saddington and Kilby Roads was unavoidable. The red brick solidity of the houses, clearly seen in the photograph, presents an almost urban face, with gardens to the road. Many of the houses have date plaques, and virtually all fall into a range between 1890-1910. Apart from a certain tidying up of the grass verges, the provision of a footpath and the insertion of a bungalow, the view remains static.

Earl Shilton, The Hollow c1965 E161003
Earl Shilton and Barwell to its southwest have each expanded until they have literally become one, and soon a link will be made with Hinckley, about two miles further on.
Not beautiful, this long village/town was the heart of the framework knitting industry in the early to mid 19th century. By the end of the 19th century, boot and shoe factories had been built, but sadly comparatively little physical evidence remains of Earl Shilton's industrial past, apart from some late factory buildings.

GROBY, THE VILLAGE c1960 G220003
A lovely composition of local stone cottages in the lee of the tree-shrouded parish church. They rely on simple but excellent details, such as the timber-bracketed door hood and an unusual cantilevered canted bay window prominent to the right - no incongruous plastic windows and doors in 1960. The modern expansion of Groby as a Leicester suburb is to be glimpsed as the main road swings to the right towards Coalville. In front of the church is a three-storey tower which forms a part of the basically 15th-century Old Hall.

KIBWORTH BEAUCHAMP, HIGH STREET c1955 K119006
Beauchamp was added to the original name of Kibworth through Walter de Beauchamp around 1130. The red brick village, which has expanded to become interesting rather than beautiful, has excellent examples of Leicestershire vernacular, from the 17th-century Stuart House in Station Street to the well-proportioned late 19th-century small houses in the photograph. Kibworth, although large, is a village to see on foot, combining it with Kibworth Harcourt on the opposite side of the A6.

Kibworth Beauchamp, Church Road c1955 K119013
This view, taken from the north-west angle of St Wistan's churchyard, shows an uncomfortable blend of small scale 18th- and 19th-century cottages with the more angular, bland 20th-century buildings. It is an unusual piece of town-scape, which with the passage of time has been simply neatened up rather than transformed.

Kibworth Beauchamp, Station Street c1955 K119017
A typical station approach of late 19th-century houses and the aptly named Railway pub. The pretty white brick station building with its cast iron latticed windows is situated out of shot to the left and seems, at the end of the 20th century, to be empty and disused. The pretty eclectic range of 1880s cottages on the left remain virtually unaltered, as do the buildings on the right.

KIBWORTH BEAUCHAMP
The Grammar School, School Road c1955 K119010
This was one of the finest grammar schools in Leicestershire. The photograph shows the rear of the red brick master's house of c1725, which was originally of two stories until a third was added around 1835, backed by a neat garden and tennis courts. In 1965, Anthony Crosland, Labour's then Secretary of State for Education, swore that if it was the last thing he did he would destroy every grammar school in England, Wales and Northern Ireland. Leicester City and the County were pleased to put their backs into the task and they have rid themselves of schools which have yet to be replaced. The Master's House is now a well-ordered private residence, and the gardens have suburban fencing divisions. The tennis courts are a car park.

KIBWORTH HARCOURT, ALBERT ROAD c1955 K171029
Harcourt is taken from Harcourt in Normandy, and from Robert de Harewecurt, who held the village in 1202. The photograph looks at the original village centre, with the Old House immediately behind the camera, and the parish pump out of shot to the right. The Manor House on the right developed through a number of centuries from a small timber-framed structure, which remains in part. Kibworth Harcourt is somewhat more picturesque than its mother village.

KIBWORTH HARCOURT, THE OLD HOUSE c1955 K171016
The Old House of 1678 is a prominently-sited example of English domestic architecture at its very best. It is a double-pile brick building with archetypal cross-casement windows and stone dressings. The Parker coat of arms ornaments the broken-scrolled pediment. Two oeil-de-boeufs and a later Tuscan-columned porch complete this quite picturesque composition.

KIBWORTH HARCOURT, ALBERT STREET c1955 K171030

At the end of the 20th century unfortunate changes were inflicted upon this view. The houses on the left have been altered and added to in a reasonably complimentary manner, but to the right the mature trees have gone, and the 18th-century garden wall has mostly been demolished to form a new entrance to the Old House. Beyond, an enclave of unspectacular houses has been pushed in - not a particularly happy transformation. Note the unusual fret-cut timber canopy on the late 18th-century house in the centre of the photograph.

KIBWORTH HARCOURT, LEICESTER ROAD c1955 K171015

Excellent 18th-century houses are to be found on the Leicester Road, but here we see a contrast between the thatched cottages of pre-18th-century date and the Rose and Crown pub, an early roadhouse. The main road which neatly divides the two Kibworths was not put in until 1810, having previously followed the rather tortuous line of the main village street. Since 1955 little has changed in the view, apart from the pub, which adopted a somewhat brighter image.

KIBWORTH HARCOURT, THE OLD MILL c1955 K171033
The last post-mill in the county, dated 1711, it blends with the owner/managers house and the store shed to provide a self-contained industrial group. This type of mill predates tower and smock mills, utilizing the simple principal of following the wind by revolving the body of the building round a fixed central post. These mills were weatherboarded for lightness. The mounds which often supported them can sometimes be clearly seen close to deserted or shrunken village sites. The mill was last used in 1912.

KILBY, MAIN STREET c1965 K125013
From opposite the Dog and Gun Pub, the camera looks along the straight village street with its assortment of restrained houses, hedges and walls. The scene has changed little over the years apart from rather drastic alterations to the houses on the right of the photograph. The Church of St Mary Magdalen - by the locally-born architect Henry Goddard (1813-1899) - dates from 1858, and is designed in a granite-faced 13th-century style, really only to be visited by the most ardent enthusiast of Victorian architecture.

KILBY, MAIN STREET c1965 K125003
Kilby is a small street village set in an agricultural landscape of straight hawthorn hedges between Fleckney and Countesthorpe, to the south of the city. The view looks at what amounts to 19th-century small scale ribbon development along the Fleckney Road. The whole adds up to a very cordial rural scene, so common over southern Leicestershire.

Kirby Muxloe

The Castle, Main Street c1965 K126004

If one has time to glance westward, the castle is just visible from the M1 motorway as it heads northward into the Charnwood Forest. In fact, the castle is a fortified manor house, carefully set out within a rectangular moat, and the beauty of the remains, which are in the guardianship of English Heritage, resides not so much in the architecture but in the glowing colour of the brick-work, which was produced probably close to the site under the supervision of John Eles. Built by Lord Hastings of Ashby-de-la-Zouch around 1480, the castle matches in quality the brickwork of the better preserved Tattershall Castle in Lincolnshire. Poor Lord Hastings really had no time to enjoy his new house, as he carelessly managed to lose his head in 1483.

NEWTON HARCOURT, WISTOW HALL c1960 F134009
With the parish church, the Hall stands on the deserted medieval village of Wistow, about half a mile to the south of Newton Harcourt. Although retaining the form of an earlier 17th-century house, the building is essentially a drastic remodelling of 1814 by Sir Henry Halford, formally Henry Vaughan, a successful medical practitioner whose patients included members of the royal family. The rendered exterior is interesting rather than beautiful. In 1960 the Hall was in part converted to flats.

NEWTON HARCOURT, WISTOW HALL c1965 K125004
Wistow Hall sits comfortably by its artificial lake, even though Wistow Road, from Kilby to Kibworth Harcourt, runs directly past the front door. The church of St Wistan, which appears to have been remodelled in the mid 18th century, is of considerable interest for its rare, complete interior fittings of that date, enhanced by a number of good but unattributed monuments.

Newtown Linford, The Village c1965 N96001
Ribbon development of local stone houses under thatched and slated roofs, while not overheating the blood, do present a well-ordered scene; their dates range from the pre-17th century to modern, close to the parish church and the entrance to Bradgate Park. The parish pump, where the village must have originated in c 1293, is just out of shot to the left of the photograph. The small shop to the extreme right has been converted to residential use.

Newtown Linford, Bradgate Park c1965 N96012
Bradgate, a park of 820 acres, was enclosed out of Charnwood Forest in c1200 as a hunting park, and it did indeed produce very fine venison. Started around 1490 by Thomas Grey. 1st Marquis of Dorset, and built using bricks produced on the site, the house was the county's first true country house. By 1696 it and its formal gardens had developed to such quality that William III was pleased to be entertained here. It was, of course, the birth-place of Lady Jane Grey, the ill fated nine-days queen, who was executed in the Tower of London in 1554. The house fell into ruin after the 1730s when the family left, although the chapel has been preserved under a modern roof.

ROTHLEY, OLD COTTAGES, FOWKE STREET c1955 R259011
Rothley lies some five miles to the north of Leicester and to the west of the busy A6. Although the village is close to the river Soar, it was not until the arrival of the railway that it began to expand. The medieval core is rich in vernacular houses, and this atmospheric photograph shows a quite excellent example. A rather thin box-frame on the left is alongside what appears to be an 18th-century house, while opposite is a fine, close-studded pair of cottages. While not untouched, modern intrusion has been light and sensitive.

ROTHLEY, OLD COTTAGES, FOWKE STREET c1965 R259017
Now observe the same buildings overtaken by the urge to tidy up our villages as they shift their emphasis from the land toward the city. Cottages become the retreats of young executives, and thus the ugly chocolate box Grange Dairy makes its appearance. Planting in front of buildings is spirited away, while the buildings themselves are smartened up with a coat of white paint and the application of fake shutters. On the left, neat brick steps and safe pavements replace the more attractive ramped paving. Conservation area legislation should be modelled to regulate this continuous erosion of character, but regrettably it has little power in its everyday form to prevent anything short of demolition.

Smeeton Westerby, The Main Street Looking South c1955 S742009

This is an attractive village ranged along its north-south street about a mile to the south of Kibworth Beauchamp. Prior to its being enclosed, a more complicated street pattern was in place, with Mill Lane linking to Fleckney and Debdale Lane to Foxton. The photograph exudes a quiet rural atmosphere which is little changed. The fine house closing the view and the cottages in general remain readily recognisable. A single regret is the free importation of plastic windows, which strike a discordant note.

South Wigston, Blaby Road c1965 S548024

As late as 1870, enclosure meadowland and hawthorn hedges stretched away from Wigston, but the ensuing period up to 1900 was to see a trebling of population figures as hosiers and boot and shoe manufacturers from Leicester moved in. Workers took up residence on a grid-iron of industrial streets, and the town boomed. This view along the Main Street, apart from the unattractive 1950s buildings in the foreground, looks beyond to the earlier Conservative Club and the Congregational Church; above the trees the protruding lead spike of St Thomas's Church (1893) by Stockdale Harrison can be seen, bringing together probably the best architectural group in the town.

SOUTH WIGSTON
Countesthorpe Road c1960 S548003
No-one could pretend that this scene is one of romantic beauty, but this long row of late 19th-century terraced houses with its excellent corner shop has a well mannered charm. Bootscrapers, timber-sashed windows and moulded brick arched heads to the ground floor windows and doors provide a quality so often lacking in modern housing. Sadly, every brick and tile has gone, to make space in true Wigston style for an open car park.

SOUTH WIGSTON, COUNTESTHORPE ROAD c1955 S548005

The three-storey framed building on the left must have been very new when this photograph was taken. As Alpha House, it remains little changed, along with its close neighbour, St Mary's Roman Catholic Church. The major change is confined to the introduction of industrial units on the semi-open ground to the right. As in almost every other photograph, the lack of cars is striking.

SOUTH WIGSTON, FAIRFIELD SHOPPING CENTRE, GLOUCESTER CRESCENT c1960 S548014

A rather flowery title for a small shopping development of the late 1950s on the Fairfield Estate, away to the east of the town's main shopping street. As a range of handy local shops the group continues in business, although the end unit, which was empty around 1960, continues to be empty some forty years later.

South Wigston, Crow Mill c1960 S548008
Situated on the river Sence to the south of the town, the mill was first recorded around the mid 12th century, and by the early 17th century a windmill had also been built a little to its north. The photograph shows a probably 18th-century brick shell in a setting of hawthorns and reedy water. The owners of the nearby Grand Union Canal bought the mill around 1820, installing a steam engine, but after about 1900 all milling seems to have ceased. The building was later converted to residential use.

South Wigston, The Grand Union Canal c1960 S548019
The Grand Union Canal was extended from Leicester to Market Harborough via the dramatic locks at Foxton in 1809. What better place to be when a period of quiet contemplation is the order of the day? The shelter of the great hawthorn hedges, the silent rippling movement of the water and the stillness of the reeds and trees produces that so-elusive sound of silence, often longed for but rarely experienced.

SWITHLAND, THE VILLAGE c1955 S550001
The picturesque village is situated on a minor east-west road, rising up from the reservoir past Sir James Pennethorne's hall, which took some twenty years to complete, the medieval parish church and on to Woodhouse Eaves. The Tudoresque cottages of c1840, with their drip moulds and lattice windows, make an attractive composition which has changed little. Of interest are the heavy slate boundary walls between the buildings.

SYSTON, HIGH STREET c1955 S488008
An attractive corner of medieval Sithestan (1254). The house which forms the angle with Chapel Street on the left is pre-17th-century, lately repainted and rethatched. The turn of the century Bull's Head pub is now in use as the Syston District Social Club; as is so common in the village, over half the buildings in the middle distance have gone to make way for unattractive 1970s replacements. Adjacent to the thatched house is an excellent early 19th-century three-storey red brick residence which overlooks The Green on its south side.

SYSTON, THE GREEN c1955 S488009

The 15th-century local granite and limestone church tower of St Peter and St Paul shows above the low rise houses which bound The Green; it was heavily 'restored' in 1872 by F W Ordish. He also made additions to Leicester's Corn Exchange, and 'restored' St Michael's Church, Rearsby, 1858, in a heavy-handed fashion. Although devoid of good monuments, the interior is of some interest. In the churchyard are a number of simple local slate headstones of considerable calligraphic quality; they remain upright and, praise be, have not been used as paving slabs.

SYSTON, THE GREEN c1955 S488010

It must have been a considerable worry at council meetings when plans were discussed for this attractive open area, bounded by houses of quality ranging from thatches of the 17th century and earlier, to flat brick fronts of the early 19th century. So, instead of opting for a sensitive pedestrian and architecture-friendly scheme, the area is now transformed into a peculiarly urban landscape, half car park and half odd seating which one would hesitate to use. All in all, it blends with the remainder of this unfortunate village.

SYSTON

Melton Road c1955 S488007

How did it happen? Syston, a Domesday village situated about four miles north of Leicester, was industrialised by an influx of framework knitters in the 19th century, which generated standardised red brick buildings of neat and unobtrusive design. Even the cinema of the 1930s on the right is in relative harmony with its surroundings. It is not, in fact, until after the Second World War that the village became devastated by planning ineptness. In place of the cinema is now an ill-designed single-storey supermarket with a similar building next door, and this pattern extends its tentacles into the heart of the village until it is spoiled. W G Hoskins refers to Syston as 'a large and ugly industrial village', but in reality this is, in fact, a post-1945 disaster.

WIGSTON, TOWN CENTRE c1965 W366032
The design of the building on the extreme left of the photograph is 'restrained Co-op' of the 1930s, not picturesque but solid and honest. Beyond are the utilitarian shops of the 1960s, quite new when the picture was taken. Today much has gone, including the odd eaves-slatted canopy to the recessed shops, which has been sawn off. The Co-op has been rebuilt in a modern grey brick and glazed tile of about 1980. At least the later 19th-century backdrop buildings remain in situ.

WIGSTON, BELL STREET c1965 W366040
Looking towards Bull Head Street, a mixture of building periods come together to provide a pleasant moment in Wigston. The Queen's Head Pub of the late 19th century is next door to the mid-20th-century house, with to the left and right two-storey shops. From this perspective the scene has changed little, but look behind the camera and there is all the poor quality 1960s buildings that one could ever wish to see!

Wigston, Leicester Road looking North c1960 W366042

This architecture is not exciting, but very user-friendly: a corner shop with others adjacent, each with their good timber fronts, and on the opposite side of the road The Bell pub, making up a standard local group. In the distance lurks the precursor of Wigston's architectural doom in the form of a less attractive newcomer of the later 1950s. Now, apart from the pub, all has been cleared away, needless to say to provide sites for more drab 1960s development. There is nothing more to be said.

Wigston, The Fire Station, Bull Head Street c1965 W366038

The pleasant later 19th-century houses look across at the cleared site upon which the Fire Station and the garage (once Regent, now Texaco) were built around the late 1950s. The fire station is typical of its kind with its curving roof, jettied first floor and flat-roofed flanking engine park. Behind the camera on rising ground is St Wolstans Church, vainly trying to ignore its insensitive dual carriageway setting.

WOODHOUSE EAVES
Main Street c1955 W367051
Situated in the forest of Charnwood, which was probably uninhabited prior to 1086, Woodhouse Eaves, with its close neighbour Swithland, is associated with the vast output of slate during the 18th and 19th centuries. Used as roofing material and for graveyard headstones, it has the ability to take the most intricate carving and to weather supremely well. Since 1955 the village as a whole has undergone subtle changes rather than a blatant remodelling. The parish pump is situated out of shot to the right, the Hovis sign and shop has been replaced by a more elaborate chemist's premises, and some cottages have gone, but the Pear Tree Pub continues to cater for human needs. The prominent many-branched telegraph pole is now a truncated spike.

Woodhouse Eaves, The Village c1955 W367044

A picturesque view, whose general outlook has altered quite radically since 1955. St Paul's school to the left, dating from 1835 with its Tudoresque details and gable end bell-cote, has changed dramatically to become a residential property. The entrance door remains in situ, but the stone mullion and transom windows have gone in favour of unattractive modern replacements; strangely, the bell-cote now resides in the garden of School House on the opposite side of the road. Little boxes now cover the treed backdrop, and the Esso garage has, unfortunately, become a gaudy exercise in eye-catching commercialism.

WOODHOUSE EAVES, MAIN STREET c1955 W367049

The street rises away from the village centre, past what is now the village hall on the left. In the photograph this attractive local stone building is enhanced by its cast iron latticed windows and porch, both now gone. The character of the hall has been negated at a single stroke, presumably through the need to carefully repaint the old windows, whereas the new ones require somewhat less effort.

WOODHOUSE EAVES, CHARNWOOD FOREST CHILDREN'S CONVALESCENT HOME c 1955 W367011

This is a large Edwardian house on the south side of the village, with its balcony and rows of sashed windows, just far enough out of the city. In 1955, this was as good as a holiday. To be ill as a child a decade after the war was considered worthwhile if it meant being allowed to recuperate at the Home. It was, however, always just as good to return home again.

Index

Frith Book Co Titles

www.francisfrith.co.uk

The Frith Book Company publishes over 100 new titles each year. A selection of those currently available are listed below. For latest catalogue please contact Frith Book Co.

Town Books 96pages, approx 100 photos. County and Themed Books 128 pages, approx 150 photos (unless specified). All titles hardback laminated case and jacket except those indicated pb (paperback)

Amersham, Chesham & Rickmansworth (pb)	1-85937-340-2	£9.99
Ancient Monuments & Stone Circles	1-85937-143-4	£17.99
Aylesbury (pb)	1-85937-227-9	£9.99
Bakewell	1-85937-113-2	£12.99
Barnstaple (pb)	1-85937-300-3	£9.99
Bath (pb)	1-85937419-0	£9.99
Bedford (pb)	1-85937-205-8	£9.99
Berkshire (pb)	1-85937-191-4	£9.99
Berkshire Churches	1-85937-170-1	£17.99
Blackpool (pb)	1-85937-382-8	£9.99
Bognor Regis (pb)	1-85937-431-x	£9.99
Bournemouth	1-85937-067-5	£12.99
Bradford (pb)	1-85937-204-x	£9.99
Brighton & Hove(pb)	1-85937-192-2	£8.99
Bristol (pb)	1-85937-264-3	£9.99
British Life A Century Ago (pb)	1-85937-213-9	£9.99
Buckinghamshire (pb)	1-85937-200-7	£9.99
Camberley (pb)	1-85937-222-8	£9.99
Cambridge (pb)	1-85937-422-0	£9.99
Cambridgeshire (pb)	1-85937-420-4	£9.99
Canals & Waterways (pb)	1-85937-291-0	£9.99
Canterbury Cathedral (pb)	1-85937-179-5	£9.99
Cardiff (pb)	1-85937-093-4	£9.99
Carmarthenshire	1-85937-216-3	£14.99
Chelmsford (pb)	1-85937-310-0	£9.99
Cheltenham (pb)	1-85937-095-0	£9.99
Cheshire (pb)	1-85937-271-6	£9.99
Chester	1-85937-090-x	£12.99
Chesterfield	1-85937-378-x	£9.99
Chichester (pb)	1-85937-228-7	£9.99
Colchester (pb)	1-85937-188-4	£8.99
Cornish Coast	1-85937-163-9	£14.99
Cornwall (pb)	1-85937-229-5	£9.99
Cornwall Living Memories	1-85937-248-1	£14.99
Cotswolds (pb)	1-85937-230-9	£9.99
Cotswolds Living Memories	1-85937-255-4	£14.99
County Durham	1-85937-123-x	£14.99
Croydon Living Memories	1-85937-162-0	£9.99
Cumbria	1-85937-101-9	£14.99
Dartmoor	1-85937-145-0	£14.99
Derby (pb)	1-85937-367-4	£9.99
Derbyshire (pb)	1-85937-196-5	£9.99
Devon (pb)	1-85937-297-x	£9.99
Dorset (pb)	1-85937-269-4	£9.99
Dorset Churches	1-85937-172-8	£17.99
Dorset Coast (pb)	1-85937-299-6	£9.99
Dorset Living Memories	1-85937-210-4	£14.99
Down the Severn	1-85937-118-3	£14.99
Down the Thames (pb)	1-85937-278-3	£9.99
Down the Trent	1-85937-311-9	£14.99
Dublin (pb)	1-85937-231-7	£9.99
East Anglia (pb)	1-85937-265-1	£9.99
East London	1-85937-080-2	£14.99
East Sussex	1-85937-130-2	£14.99
Eastbourne	1-85937-061-6	£12.99
Edinburgh (pb)	1-85937-193-0	£8.99
England in the 1880s	1-85937-331-3	£17.99
English Castles (pb)	1-85937-434-4	£9.99
English Country Houses	1-85937-161-2	£17.99
Essex (pb)	1-85937-270-8	£9.99
Exeter	1-85937-126-4	£12.99
Exmoor	1-85937-132-9	£14.99
Falmouth	1-85937-066-7	£12.99
Folkestone (pb)	1-85937-124-8	£9.99
Glasgow (pb)	1-85937-190-6	£9.99
Gloucestershire	1-85937-102-7	£14.99
Great Yarmouth (pb)	1-85937-426-3	£9.99
Greater Manchester (pb)	1-85937-266-x	£9.99
Guildford (pb)	1-85937-410-7	£9.99
Hampshire (pb)	1-85937-279-1	£9.99
Hampshire Churches (pb)	1-85937-207-4	£9.99
Harrogate	1-85937-423-9	£9.99
Hastings & Bexhill (pb)	1-85937-131-0	£9.99
Heart of Lancashire (pb)	1-85937-197-3	£9.99
Helston (pb)	1-85937-214-7	£9.99
Hereford (pb)	1-85937-175-2	£9.99
Herefordshire	1-85937-174-4	£14.99
Hertfordshire (pb)	1-85937-247-3	£9.99
Horsham (pb)	1-85937-432-8	£9.99
Humberside	1-85937-215-5	£14.99
Hythe, Romney Marsh & Ashford	1-85937-256-2	£9.99

Available from your local bookshop or from the publisher

Frith Book Co Titles (continued)

Title	ISBN	Price
Ipswich (pb)	1-85937-424-7	£9.99
Ireland (pb)	1-85937-181-7	£9.99
Isle of Man (pb)	1-85937-268-6	£9.99
Isles of Scilly	1-85937-136-1	£14.99
Isle of Wight (pb)	1-85937-429-8	£9.99
Isle of Wight Living Memories	1-85937-304-6	£14.99
Kent (pb)	1-85937-189-2	£9.99
Kent Living Memories	1-85937-125-6	£14.99
Lake District (pb)	1-85937-275-9	£9.99
Lancaster, Morecambe & Heysham (pb)	1-85937-233-3	£9.99
Leeds (pb)	1-85937-202-3	£9.99
Leicester	1-85937-073-x	£12.99
Leicestershire (pb)	1-85937-185-x	£9.99
Lincolnshire (pb)	1-85937-433-6	£9.99
Liverpool & Merseyside (pb)	1-85937-234-1	£9.99
London (pb)	1-85937-183-3	£9.99
Ludlow (pb)	1-85937-176-0	£9.99
Luton (pb)	1-85937-235-x	£9.99
Maidstone	1-85937-056-x	£14.99
Manchester (pb)	1-85937-198-1	£9.99
Middlesex	1-85937-158-2	£14.99
New Forest	1-85937-128-0	£14.99
Newark (pb)	1-85937-366-6	£9.99
Newport, Wales (pb)	1-85937-258-9	£9.99
Newquay (pb)	1-85937-421-2	£9.99
Norfolk (pb)	1-85937-195-7	£9.99
Norfolk Living Memories	1-85937-217-1	£14.99
Northamptonshire	1-85937-150-7	£14.99
Northumberland Tyne & Wear (pb)	1-85937-281-3	£9.99
North Devon Coast	1-85937-146-9	£14.99
North Devon Living Memories	1-85937-261-9	£14.99
North London	1-85937-206-6	£14.99
North Wales (pb)	1-85937-298-8	£9.99
North Yorkshire (pb)	1-85937-236-8	£9.99
Norwich (pb)	1-85937-194-9	£8.99
Nottingham (pb)	1-85937-324-0	£9.99
Nottinghamshire (pb)	1-85937-187-6	£9.99
Oxford (pb)	1-85937-411-5	£9.99
Oxfordshire (pb)	1-85937-430-1	£9.99
Peak District (pb)	1-85937-280-5	£9.99
Penzance	1-85937-069-1	£12.99
Peterborough (pb)	1-85937-219-8	£9.99
Piers	1-85937-237-6	£17.99
Plymouth	1-85937-119-1	£12.99
Poole & Sandbanks (pb)	1-85937-251-1	£9.99
Preston (pb)	1-85937-212-0	£9.99
Reading (pb)	1-85937-238-4	£9.99
Romford (pb)	1-85937-319-4	£9.99
Salisbury (pb)	1-85937-239-2	£9.99
Scarborough (pb)	1-85937-379-8	£9.99
St Albans (pb)	1-85937-341-0	£9.99
St Ives (pb)	1-85937415-8	£9.99
Scotland (pb)	1-85937-182-5	£9.99
Scottish Castles (pb)	1-85937-323-2	£9.99
Sevenoaks & Tunbridge	1-85937-057-8	£12.99
Sheffield, South Yorks (pb)	1-85937-267-8	£9.99
Shrewsbury (pb)	1-85937-325-9	£9.99
Shropshire (pb)	1-85937-326-7	£9.99
Somerset	1-85937-153-1	£14.99
South Devon Coast	1-85937-107-8	£14.99
South Devon Living Memories	1-85937-168-x	£14.99
South Hams	1-85937-220-1	£14.99
Southampton (pb)	1-85937-427-1	£9.99
Southport (pb)	1-85937-425-5	£9.99
Staffordshire	1-85937-047-0	£12.99
Stratford upon Avon	1-85937-098-5	£12.99
Suffolk (pb)	1-85937-221-x	£9.99
Suffolk Coast	1-85937-259-7	£14.99
Surrey (pb)	1-85937-240-6	£9.99
Sussex (pb)	1-85937-184-1	£9.99
Swansea (pb)	1-85937-167-1	£9.99
Tees Valley & Cleveland	1-85937-211-2	£14.99
Thanet (pb)	1-85937-116-7	£9.99
Tiverton (pb)	1-85937-178-7	£9.99
Torbay	1-85937-063-2	£12.99
Truro	1-85937-147-7	£12.99
Victorian and Edwardian Cornwall	1-85937-252-x	£14.99
Victorian & Edwardian Devon	1-85937-253-8	£14.99
Victorian & Edwardian Kent	1-85937-149-3	£14.99
Vic & Ed Maritime Album	1-85937-144-2	£17.99
Victorian and Edwardian Sussex	1-85937-157-4	£14.99
Victorian & Edwardian Yorkshire	1-85937-154-x	£14.99
Victorian Seaside	1-85937-159-0	£17.99
Villages of Devon (pb)	1-85937-293-7	£9.99
Villages of Kent (pb)	1-85937-294-5	£9.99
Villages of Sussex (pb)	1-85937-295-3	£9.99
Warwickshire (pb)	1-85937-203-1	£9.99
Welsh Castles (pb)	1-85937-322-4	£9.99
West Midlands (pb)	1-85937-289-9	£9.99
West Sussex	1-85937-148-5	£14.99
West Yorkshire (pb)	1-85937-201-5	£9.99
Weymouth (pb)	1-85937-209-0	£9.99
Wiltshire (pb)	1-85937-277-5	£9.99
Wiltshire Churches (pb)	1-85937-171-x	£9.99
Wiltshire Living Memories	1-85937-245-7	£14.99
Winchester (pb)	1-85937-428-x	£9.99
Windmills & Watermills	1-85937-242-2	£17.99
Worcester (pb)	1-85937-165-5	£9.99
Worcestershire	1-85937-152-3	£14.99
York (pb)	1-85937-199-x	£9.99
Yorkshire (pb)	1-85937-186-8	£9.99
Yorkshire Living Memories	1-85937-166-3	£14.99

See Frith books on the internet www.francisfrith.co.uk

Frith Products & Services

Francis Frith would doubtless be pleased to know that the pioneering publishing venture he started in 1860 still continues today. A hundred and forty years later, The Francis Frith Collection continues in the same innovative tradition and is now one of the foremost publishers of vintage photographs in the world. Some of the current activities include:

Interior Decoration

Today Frith's photographs can be seen framed and as giant wall murals in thousands of pubs, restaurants, hotels, banks, retail stores and other public buildings throughout the country. In every case they enhance the unique local atmosphere of the places they depict and provide reminders of gentler days in an increasingly busy and frenetic world.

Product Promotions

Frith products are used by many major companies to promote the sales of their own products or to reinforce their own history and heritage. Frith promotions have been used by Hovis bread, Courage beers, Scots Porage Oats, Colman's mustard, Cadbury's foods, Mellow Birds coffee, Dunhill pipe tobacco, Guinness, and Bulmer's Cider.

Genealogy and Family History

As the interest in family history and roots grows world-wide, more and more people are turning to Frith's photographs of Great Britain for images of the towns, villages and streets where their ancestors lived; and, of course, photographs of the churches and chapels where their ancestors were christened, married and buried are an essential part of every genealogy tree and family album.

Frith Products

All Frith photographs are available Framed or just as Mounted Prints and Posters (size 23 x 16 inches). These may be ordered from the address below. From time to time other products - Address Books, Calendars, Table Mats, etc - are available.

The Internet

Already twenty thousand Frith photographs can be viewed and purchased on the internet through the Frith websites and a myriad of partner sites.

For more detailed information on Frith companies and products, look at these sites:

www.francisfrith.co.uk
www.francisfrith.com
(for North American visitors)

See the complete list of Frith Books at:

www.francisfrith.co.uk

This web site is regularly updated with the latest list of publications from the Frith Book Company. If you wish to buy books relating to another part of the country that your local bookshop does not stock, you may purchase on-line.

For further information, trade, or author enquiries please contact us at the address below:
The Francis Frith Collection, Frith's Barn, Teffont, Salisbury, Wiltshire, England SP3 5QP.
Tel: +44 (0)1722 716 376 Fax: +44 (0)1722 716 881 Email: sales@francisfrith.co.uk

See Frith books on the internet www.francisfrith.co.uk

TO RECEIVE YOUR FREE MOUNTED PRINT

Mounted Print
Overall size 14 x 11 inches

Cut out this Voucher and return it with your remittance for £1.95 to cover postage and handling, to UK addresses. For overseas addresses please include £4.00 post and handling.
Choose any photograph included in this book. Your SEPIA print will be A4 in size, and mounted in a cream mount with burgundy rule line, overall size 14 x 11 inches.

Order additional Mounted Prints at HALF PRICE (only £7.49 each*)
If there are further pictures you would like to order, possibly as gifts for friends and family, purchase them at half price (no additional postage and handling required).

Have your Mounted Prints framed*
For an additional £14.95 per print you can have your chosen Mounted Print framed in an elegant polished wood and gilt moulding, overall size 16 x 13 inches (no additional postage and handling required).

*** IMPORTANT!**
These special prices are only available if ordered using the original voucher on this page (no copies permitted) and at the same time as your free Mounted Print, for delivery to the same address

Frith Collectors' Guild

From time to time we publish a magazine of news and stories about Frith photographs and further special offers of Frith products. If you would like 12 months FREE membership, please return this form.

Send completed forms to:
The Francis Frith Collection, Frith's Barn, Teffont, Salisbury, Wiltshire SP3 5QP

Voucher for FREE and Reduced Price Frith Prints

Picture no.	Page number	Qty	Mounted @ £7.49	Framed + £14.95	Total Cost
		1	**Free of charge***	£	£
			£7.49	£	£
			£7.49	£	£
			£7.49	£	£
			£7.49	£	£
			£7.49	£	£
Please allow 28 days for delivery				*** Post & handling**	**£1.95**
Book Title				**Total Order Cost**	**£**

Please do not photocopy this voucher. Only the original is valid, so please cut it out and return it to us.

I enclose a cheque / postal order for £ ....
made payable to 'The Francis Frith Collection'
OR please debit my Mastercard / Visa / Switch / Amex card
(credit cards please on all overseas orders)

Number ....
Issue No (Switch only) .... Valid from (Amex/Switch) ....
Expires .... Signature ....

Name Mr/Mrs/Ms ....
Address ....
....
....
.... Postcode ....
Daytime Tel No .... Valid to 31/12/02

The Francis Frith Collectors' Guild

Please enrol me as a member for 12 months free of charge.

Name Mr/Mrs/Ms ....
Address ....
....
....
.... Postcode ....

Free Print - see overleaf

Would you like to find out more about Francis Frith?

We have recently recruited some entertaining speakers who are happy to visit local groups, clubs and societies to give an illustrated talk documenting Frith's travels and photographs. If you are a member of such a group and are interested in hosting a presentation, we would love to hear from you.

Our speakers bring with them a small selection of our local town and county books, together with sample prints. They are happy to take orders. A small proportion of the order value is donated to the group who have hosted the presentation. The talks are therefore an excellent way of fundraising for small groups and societies.

Can you help us with information about any of the Frith photographs in this book?

We are gradually compiling an historical record for each of the photographs in the Frith archive. It is always fascinating to find out the names of the people shown in the pictures, as well as insights into the shops, buildings and other features depicted.

If you recognize anyone in the photographs in this book, or if you have information not already included in the author's caption, do let us know. We would love to hear from you, and will try to publish it in future books or articles.

Our production team

Frith books are produced by a small dedicated team at offices in the converted Grade II listed 18th-century barn at Teffont near Salisbury, illustrated above. Most have worked with the Frith Collection for many years. All have in common one quality: they have a passion for the Frith Collection. The team is constantly expanding, but currently includes:

Jason Buck, John Buck, Douglas Burns, Heather Crisp, Isobel Hall, Rob Hames, Hazel Heaton, Peter Horne, James Kinnear, Tina Leary, Hannah Marsh, Eliza Sackett, Terence Sackett, Sandra Sanger, Shelley Tolcher, Susanna Walker, Clive Wathen and Jenny Wathen.